You Wouldn't Want to Sail on the Mary Rose!

Written by
Fiona Macdonald

Illustrated by
David Antram

Created and designed by
David Salariya

BOOK HOUSE
a SALARIYA *imprint*

Contents

Introduction

Let's travel back in time to 1545. You're a young boy from the south of England. With your father, a poor farmer, you've driven into Portsmouth with dried apples to sell. The town is buzzing with news of an invasion: French ships are approaching – fast! Henry VIII's navy has sailed to Portsmouth. The English army is there too, ready to fight. King Henry VIII has arrived to lead the defenders, and his favourite warship, the *Mary Rose*, is close by. Just look – she's splendid! Amazed and impressed, you see her pennants (flags), big guns and crew, busy on board. You can't help wondering: would I want to sail on the *Mary Rose*?

Fine sight, isn't she?

Pride of the fleet

Do you want to join a fine new fighting force: Henry VIII's navy? In the past, English rulers had to rent or borrow ships if they wanted to fight at sea. But now King Henry VIII owns about 50 well-armed vessels. *Mary Rose* is the pride of the fleet. Yesterday, 18 July 1545, King Henry met navy commanders at Portsmouth to make plans to fight the French invaders. The new navy must be ready!

Enemy ships are here, Sire, and here...

IT TAKES ALL SORTS – THE TUDOR NAVY. As well as great ships like the *Mary Rose*, Henry VIII's navy also has other vessels like these:

Galley

Galleas

Rowbarge

GALLEAS: with sails and oars, these are more manoeuvrable than the great ships. They have the guns of a galley and low castles with guns on each side.

GALLEY: large sleek vessel, with big guns at the front and a pointed 'beak' for ramming. Mostly powered by men rowing, they have a single mast.

ROWBARGE: these are smaller versions of galleasses; long with low castles at each end, three masts and a set of 15-16 oars on each side.

Phew! It's heavy! New timber for the hull!

Handy hint

First find your trees! You'll need 600 tall English oaks to build a warship like the *Mary Rose*.

BETTER THAN EVER?
Between 1536–1538, *Mary Rose* was refitted (rebuilt). Her wooden hull was strengthened and new gunports were cut in her sides. Now she's about 12 metres wide and 35 metres long, displaces 700 tonnes, and is armed with 91 guns. She has a crew of over 200 sailors plus 30 expert gunners, and can carry around 185 soldiers.

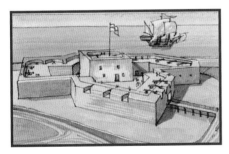

FORTS AND DOCKS. To protect England's coastline, Henry VIII has ordered new forts, including Southsea Castle near Portsmouth (above). And he's paid for new docks where warships can be built, refitted and repaired.

WARNING SIGNALS. England's coastline is dangerous. Henry VIII's new charts guide navy ships and mark the position of dangerous rocks and sandbanks.

GETTING ORGANISED. It costs a lot to run the navy. So Henry VIII has set up a new government office (called the Admiralty) to keep track of spending.

7

So you want to go to sea?

hy do you want to leave home? For adventure? To explore? Because you like big ships? Or because farm life is poor, hard and miserable? You'll find that many sailors have gone to sea because they needed money. Others have been recruited by local lords and landowners. Still more have joined ships because they were homeless or hungry. They say it's better to risk your life at sea than to starve on land!

If only...

FAMILY TRADITIONS.

You'll also meet sailors who come from seafaring families, or have parents working in trades linked to the sea, such as sail-making or fish-selling. They've grown up in busy ports around the coast. People often say: 'the sea is in their blood'.

Handy hint

Learn! Learn! Learn! Training for a skilled career is your best hope of escaping from poverty.

MUD, MUCK, SWEAT, TOIL, TEARS – and no money. Farming is a risky business. Crops can be ruined by bad weather; animals die from disease. You hope for a better career.

1

2

3

4

5

DOWN ON THE TUDOR FARM.

1. No food if crops fail.
2. Rats, fleas, deadly disease.
3. Rents and taxes to pay.
4. No help from neighbours – they're poor, and begging is banned.
5. Religious quarrels can cost you your life!

Meet the crew!

Ships at sea are closed communities. So you'll have to get on with your shipmates! They're a mixed bunch – from grand gentlemen to humble trainee sailors. They, or their ancestors, have mostly come from south-west England or from lands overseas, including Italy, Spain and North Africa. Most sailors are under 30, though some senior officers are older, but all use their skills to keep the ship sailing safely. Tudor sailors serve on merchant ships as well as warships. They simply make an agreement with a ship's bosun (officer in charge of passing the captain's orders to the crew).

It's a deal!

On the Mary Rose, you'll meet...

Captain – Vice Admiral Sir George Carew

Officers (command soldiers on board)

Pilot (guides ship in dangerous waters)

Cooks

Surgeon

Gentlemen (assist captai

You're not the youngest any more, Micah!

Handy hint

Sheets? (ropes)
Heads? (toilets)
Ships' crews speak their own strange jargon. Don't worry! Look and listen and you'll soon learn.

NOT ONLY, BUT ALSO...
Like all big ships, the *Mary Rose* relies on hundreds of suppliers on shore: from brickmakers, cobblers and victuallers (food suppliers) to rope-makers, iron-workers, gun-founders, basket-weavers, carriers and many more.

Purser (paymaster)

Musicians

Carpenters

Bosun

Ordinary sailors

Master gunner (in charge of guns)

Ship's dog

11

Do you know the ropes?

Tudor ships don't have steam or diesel engines; they've not yet been invented. Instead, they are powered by men rowing with oars, or by the wind blowing into huge canvas (thick cloth) sails. These sails are fixed to spars (long poles) hung from the ships' masts, and are raised or lowered by hauling on ropes. It's skilful work to control a sailing ship, and physically exhausting.

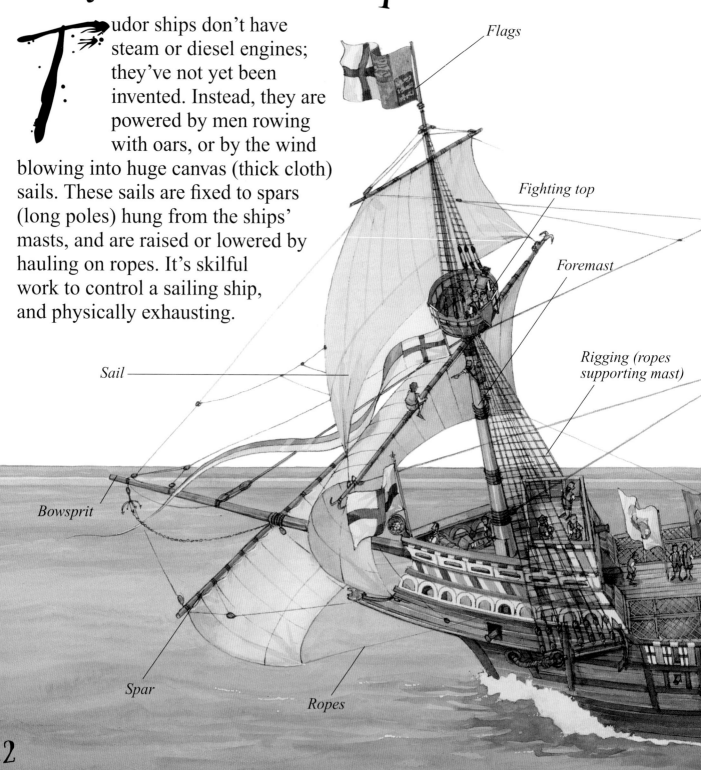

Flags

Fighting top

Foremast

Rigging (ropes supporting mast)

Sail

Bowsprit

Spar

Ropes

12

LOOK OUT on deck for swinging ropes and spars. Don't trip or slip. Try not to feel seasick – and don't fall overboard!

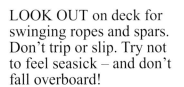

Handy hint

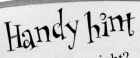

Got good eyesight? And a head for heights? Then you might be chosen as lookout, high up in the fighting top.

WHERE TO GO? There are no landmarks out on the open sea. Use a chart and a compass to plot (plan) your course. At night, check your position by observing the stars.

MEASURE TIME with a sandglass, and signal the end of watches (four-hour periods of duty) by ringing the watch bell.

HOW FAST, HOW DEEP? Check your speed by seeing how long it takes for a logline (measured length of rope) to unravel in the water. And use a rope with a weight at one end to find out the depth of the sea. You don't want to run aground!

THE CRUEL SEA. Out at sea, there are hazards all around, from rocks and reefs (1) to hurricanes and wild waves (2). Or you might be trapped, helpless and unable to move, by calms (3).

13

Are you ready for war?

They're state-of-the art. And they're very deadly! Warships like the *Mary Rose* and her sister ship the *Peter Pomegranate* are like floating gun platforms, able to destroy as well as capture. *Mary Rose*'s duty will be to lead a new type of battle: with guns at sea. In the past, attackers sailed close to enemy ships so that soldiers could leap across and fight on deck. But now *Mary Rose* has guns that fire shot (stone or iron balls) from a distance. These smash into enemy ships to make them impossible to sail and easier to capture. And they kill enemy sailors.

Look at that – the latest design!

OLD AND NEW. *Mary Rose* also carried skilled archers who shot volleys of deadly arrows down upon the enemy. It takes so much effort to use a longbow that archers get painful back and shoulder injuries.

Handy hint

Keep a bucket of urine, vinegar or sand handy! Warship crews throw firebombs at enemies to set fire to decks, rigging – and people.

▼ GET A GRIP. The *Mary Rose* also carries traditional grappling hooks. Sailors throw these to grab hold of enemy vessels, so that soldiers can leap across and fight.

Man the guns

 GET RID of all traces of previous firings. For safety, you need a clean gun.

 LOAD with fresh gunpowder. Push that right down to the end of the gun barrel.

 ADD A WAD of cloth or rags, to act as a cushion for the shot.

 ROLL the shot down the barrel. Add a tampion (wooden disc) to keep it in place.

 PULL THE GUN into position, with its muzzle poking out of the gunport.

 ADD a little priming powder – it helps the gunpowder to explode.

 FIRE THE GUN by lighting the priming powder. Stand well back...

BOOOOM! BANNNNGGGG!

SHARP SHOOTERS. Soldiers on the *Mary Rose* are armed with swords, daggers and pikes. But some also have the very latest kit: small, hand-held guns. Like big guns, these use gunpowder to fire metal shot – to kill.

Are you tough enough?

A ship is a perilous place even when it's not at sea. As a sailor, you'll risk accidents: a rolling barrel in the hold could crush you, or falling off a mast might end your life. You could die from an infected cut or catch a disease from a ship-mate (or a ship's rat or flea). Rotting food might make you sick. In wartime, enemy arrows or gun-shot will probably kill you. Do you really think you're tough and brave enough to join the *Mary Rose*?

He'll be dead by tomorrow...

THE BAD OLD DAYS. The surgeon and his assistants are in charge of all medical care on board. They are well-trained, for Tudor times. But we wouldn't want to endure their unpleasant treatments today!

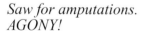

Saw for amputations. AGONY!

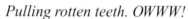

Pulling rotten teeth. OWWW!

Hot iron stops bleeding. SIZZLE!

Handy hint

Carry a comb! Lice cause horrid itching that can drive the toughest sailors mad.

KILL OR CURE. Ships' surgeons do their best but can't mend badly broken bones or cure internal injuries. They don't have drugs to fight serious infections. Some of their treatments are extremely painful. Others can kill!

Pomander hides bad smells. POOH!

TUDORS THOUGHT that disease was caused by unbalanced 'humours' (liquids) in the body, and spread by bad smells. So surgeons bled patients (took blood) to try to cure them, and carried sweet-smelling pomanders to protect against infection.

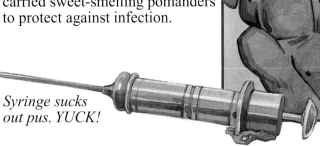

Leeches drink blood. EEK!

Syringe sucks out pus. YUCK!

Surgeons make foul-tasting potions from herbs. AARGH!

17

Do you have a strong stomach?

How would you feed hundreds of hungry men with no shops to go to? That's the task facing pursers and cooks on warships like *Mary Rose*. Before their ships set sail, pursers have to make sure that there's enough food and drink on board to last until they can be re-supplied. (Tudor water's polluted, so sailors drink up to 4 litres daily of very weak beer). Cooks have to keep all supplies fresh and safe to eat without refrigerators to help them, and prepare two meals every day, even when the ship is rolling and swaying.

Woof!

Food on board

Pickled fish – smelly!

Stewed meat and bones – grisly!

Ship's biscuit – crunchy!

Brass cauldron, brick stove - a great kitchen!

Handy hint

Dip and dunk. Ship's biscuits are baked twice to make them last longer. They're too hard to eat dry.

WANT TO WASH before eating? Grab a bucket of sea water. You'll be clean, but wet and chilly.

FOR THE TOILET sailors stand to use a 'piss-dale' or 'heads' (drain-holes in the deck). Before you go, remember to check which way the wind is blowing!

Flour for bread gets maggots – wriggly!

Apples can go rotten – squelchy!

19

Where will you rest, relax and pray?

On board the *Mary Rose*, the crew work in watches: four hours on duty, four hours off. So what will you do when you're resting or relaxing? Some of the time, you'll sleep, though that may not be easy. There's always something going on: shouted orders, sailors running, carpenters hammering, howling wind, crashing waves... Unless you're an officer, or a specialist such as the surgeon, you won't have a cabin. You'll sleep wherever you can find a space; next to the guns, perhaps, or in a corner of a deck with your cloak wrapped round you.

THERE ARE NO BEDS on board for ordinary sailors. But a heap of old sails can be cosy, as long as they are dry.

NO SOCIAL MEDIA, no streaming, no TV. Tudor sailors make their own entertainment:
1. Pipe and tabor (drum)
2. Singing and dancing
3. Favourite tunes on a fiddle
4. Jokes and riddles
5. Storytelling.

Our Father...

SAILORS FACE DEATH daily. For comfort, they say prayers. A rosary (left) helps them remember. Holy images (of angels, above) make them feel safer.

21

Are you ready to face invaders?

It's war! And England is in danger! Today, 19 July 1545, French warships have reached the sea off Portsmouth. All morning, it's been calm. But now the wind's sprung up and English ships can sail. You're on board the *Mary Rose*. Bravely, she advances, then turns sideways, with her starboard (right-hand) guns blazing. Now she's turning again, to fire guns from her port (left) side. But look! Oh no! A sudden gust of wind has caught her! Her sails billow and flap. She's swaying, tilting, leaning over...

STAND BACK! Huge guns and heavy shot roll around as the *Mary Rose* tips over. Get out of their way! They'll crush you!

TOO LATE! *Mary Rose's* gunports are still open. There's no time to close them. Help! Seawater's pouring in!

It's hard for gunners to hit their target if the ship is rolling. So keep her steady!

SAFE IN SOUTHSEA CASTLE, King Henry VIII watches his navy. He sees his great ship toppling over, and hears the cries of men on board. He's horrified!

MY HUSBAND! Lady Carew, wife of *Mary Rose*'s captain, is watching too. She faints with shock and terror.

NO ESCAPE! Up on the weather deck, soldiers can't escape by cutting through the nets stretched above their heads to stop enemies leaping on board.

YOU'RE THROWN CLEAR from the stern (back) of the *Mary Rose*. So far, you're lucky. But will you sink or swim?

Would you survive the shipwreck?

Disaster! The *Mary Rose* is sinking... Any moment, she'll be gone! And she's taking almost everyone on board – around 500 men – down with her to the bottom of the sea. They're trapped in the hold, below decks, in their cabins, on companionways (stairs) and under the nets. And they're drowning. You are one of the very few – just 35 people – who'll survive. Struggling to stay afloat in the water swirling round the wreck, you've been found by brave rescuers. Soon you'll be safe ashore.

God help us!

Grab my hand!

What sank the Mary Rose?

WAS IT a cannonball (above), fired by the French?

Handy hint

Like most English sailors, you can't swim. If you find some floating wreckage, hold tight – and hope!

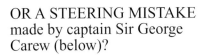

OR A STEERING MISTAKE made by captain Sir George Carew (below)?

WAS *MARY ROSE* OVERLOADED with soldiers, sailors and guns, making her unstable and likely to capsize?

WAS THE SUDDEN gust of wind that made *Mary Rose* roll and sway strong enough to blow her right over?

HAD THE REFIT, which added extra timber, made *Mary Rose* too heavy and more difficult to control?

DID THE CREW disobey the captain's orders? He was new to the *Mary Rose*. Few of her sailors had worked for him before.

WHATEVER THE REASON, *Mary Rose* sank fast, as water poured through her open gunports and flooded her hull.

Can anyone rescue your ship?

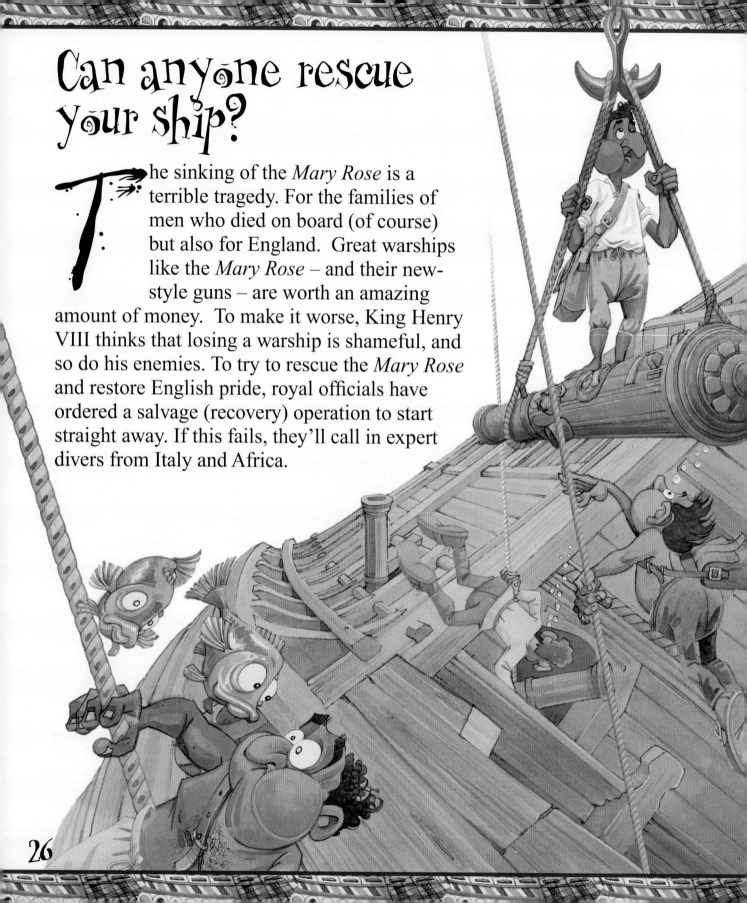

The sinking of the *Mary Rose* is a terrible tragedy. For the families of men who died on board (of course) but also for England. Great warships like the *Mary Rose* – and their new-style guns – are worth an amazing amount of money. To make it worse, King Henry VIII thinks that losing a warship is shameful, and so do his enemies. To try to rescue the *Mary Rose* and restore English pride, royal officials have ordered a salvage (recovery) operation to start straight away. If this fails, they'll call in expert divers from Italy and Africa.

Handy hint

Go to Italy, and visit the city of Venice! Some of the best divers are trained there, in warm, shallow waters.

MARY ROSE is on the sea bed. How to lift her? Divers stretch ropes to her foremast and under her hull. They hope this will help pull the *Mary Rose* upwards. Sadly their plan does not work. The foremast rope snaps and the *Mary Rose* is damaged.

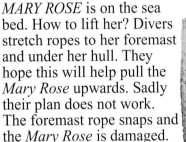

ONLY THE BEST. To salvage the *Mary Rose*, King Henry has hired expert divers. We know the names of a few of them, such as Jacques Francis. Born in Guinea, West Africa, he now works for an Italian company along with men from several different countries. So far, they've recovered some valuable guns. But *Mary Rose* herself remains underwater.

FOR CENTURIES, *Mary Rose* lay covered in mud and sand. Then in 1836, Portsmouth fishermen caught their nets on some timbers. Over the next six years, divers wearing newly-invented breathing helmets explored the wreck. They brought guns, human remains and other 'treasures' up to the surface to sell.

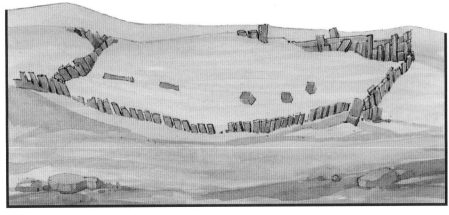

Diver in helmet, 1840s

Recovered and famous worldwide!

After the 1840s, the *Mary Rose* was 'lost' yet again. But she was not forgotten. In the 1960s, archaeologists began a fresh search, using new technology (sonar and scuba diving) to explore underwater. Imagine their excitement when, in 1971, they found some *Mary Rose* timbers! During the next 10 years, the wreck of the *Mary Rose* was very carefully excavated and recorded. Then she was raised to the surface in 1982, and preserved for us to admire – and explore. Now the *Mary Rose* is a Tudor time capsule!

MARY ROSE was tied to a metal frame, gently elevated from the seabed, then lowered into a metal cradle and raised to the surface.

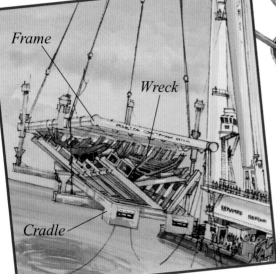

Frame

Wreck

Cradle

1. Wooden plate, bowl, spoon
2. Flask
3. Candlestick
4. Wooden tankard
5. Leather shoe

WHAT DOES the *Mary Rose* tell us? From objects found on board, we learn about life for rich and poor in Tudor times.

Handy hint

Dare to dream! The *Mary Rose* was saved thanks to the vision, courage and skill of a dedicated team.

Yes, that's right! She's over 500 years old!

FROM TIMBERS, weapons and tools found in the wreck, we learn about Tudor shipbuilding, warfare and technology.

SCIENTISTS STUDY bones and teeth from *Mary Rose*'s drowned crew to make amazing discoveries about Tudor people.

AS YOU LOOK at this great ship, stop, think and ask yourself: would I really want to sail on the *Mary Rose*?

29

Did you know?

Henry VIII's navy was multicultural. From the evidence of bones and teeth found on board the *Mary Rose*, scientists have discovered that some of her soldiers and sailors had North African and South European heritage. Documents from around the same time as the *Mary Rose* was launched also show that 3 out of every 100 Londoners had non-English origins.

So far, the remains of 179 men – and one dog – have been found on the *Mary Rose* shipwreck. Most men were between 18 and 30 years old. Two were younger than 13.

The average height of the men on the *Mary Rose* was around 165–175 cm, slightly shorter than men in England today. Many had suffered injuries, in accidents, through hard, dangerous work or from using weapons. Many also had damaged or rotten teeth.

Archaeologists think that captain Sir George Carew was probably protected by members of Henry VIII's elite royal bodyguard. They were expert archers, armed with swords and daggers. Two special bracers (wristguards), decorated with the Royal Arms, were found in the wreck of the *Mary Rose*. The ship's crew also included gentlemen officers, the bosun, the purser, a surgeon, a cook and a master carpenter, together with their assistants.

Over 19,000 objects have been recovered from the wreck of the *Mary Rose*. They range from gold coins to arrows, mail armour, carpenters' tools, wooden dishes, pewter jugs, hundreds of leather shoes, a ring, a mirror, a bosun's call (shrill whistle, used to give orders to sailors) and a chamber pot. Excavators have also found the remains of foods eaten on board, including plum stones, apple pips and 31,793 fish bones!

THE HULL of the *Mary Rose* was very fragile when it was raised from the seabed. If its timbers dried out too quickly, they would rot away. To preserve them, conservators kept them damp and washed damaging sea salt away by gently spraying water for 12 whole years! Next, a preservative wax was sprayed on to soak into the hull and strengthen it – taking another 19 years.

Finally, the *Mary Rose* was gently dried by jets of air. Today, she is kept in strictly controlled conditions. Moisture, temperature and light levels are all carefully monitored. And a splendid museum has been built as her new home.

Mary Rose timeline

1510

England's King Henry VIII orders two new warships: *Peter Pomegranate* and *Mary Rose*.

1512

Mary Rose wins race at sea; is England's fastest warship.

1520

Mary Rose is part of royal escort when Henry VIII visits French king.

1512

Mary Rose fights with new-style guns in sea battle against France.

1513

Mary Rose transports English soldiers to defeat Scots at battle of Flodden.

1522

Mary Rose is chosen as flagship (leading ship) by English admirals.

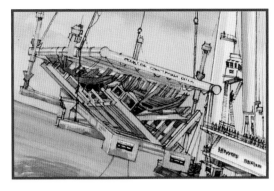

1545

French and English warships fight off Portsmouth. *Mary Rose* sinks. Most men on board drown.

1979–1982

Scientific excavation of wreck; remains of *Mary Rose* raised to the surface for study and preservation.

1536–1537

Mary Rose is refitted (rebuilt, made stronger); new gunports cut in hull.

1545–1549

Divers fail to raise wreck of *Mary Rose* but recover valuable guns.

1544

Mary Rose joins English fleet led by Henry VIII to attack northern France.

Meet the Mary Rose

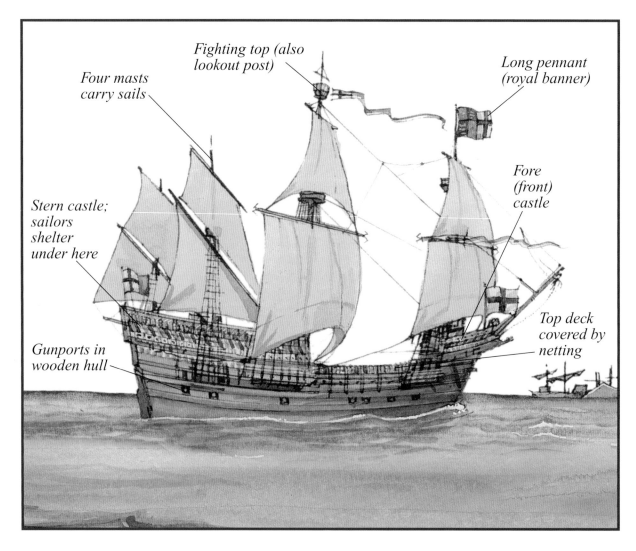

Fighting top (also lookout post)

Four masts carry sails

Long pennant (royal banner)

Stern castle; sailors shelter under here

Fore (front) castle

Gunports in wooden hull

Top deck covered by netting

Mary Rose was owned by King Henry VIII himself, not by the English nation. Henry paid for her using his own private money. That is why some of the equipment on board is marked with an 'H'. Henry took a great interest in the planning and building of ships for his new navy, especially the *Mary Rose*. He wanted her to be able to fight using the most up-to-date guns that were available.

The *Mary Rose*, from the top decks to the bottom of the hold:

CASTLES (A deck, or small tower of decks, standing on the top deck): At the bow (front) and stern (back) of the ship. Each contains decks and cabins. There is a covered space underneath the stern castle, where officers shelter from the weather and sleep.

TOP DECK/WEATHER DECK: This is open to the wind, rain and sea spray. It's where soldiers will fight hand-to-hand, old-style, if enemies board the *Mary Rose*. It's protected by strong netting stretched right across it.

MAIN DECK: The biggest guns are here with their gunports; seven on each side of the hull. There are also cabins for ship's officers, like the surgeon and the pilot. Expert carpenters, who mend and maintain the ship, have a cabin here, and stores for their woodworking tools.

ORLOP DECK: Below the main deck and above the hold. Used to store food, spare sails, ropes and other ship's equipment.

HOLD: Right at the bottom. The kitchen is here, and ballast (stones or shingle to make the *Mary Rose* more stable) and the bilge pumps. These get rid of the dirty water that collects at the bottom of the hold.

Travel, trade, adventure, war

In Tudor times, European ships and sailors travelled further and faster than ever before, to explore, to trade and to fight. The first-ever voyage around the world, by Portuguese captain Ferdinand Magellan and his crew, was made in 1519–1522, just a few years after *Mary Rose* was launched in 1511.

Mary Rose was a carrack, a ship with a deep hull and four masts that carried nine or ten huge sails. Carracks were designed to transport heavy cargoes in rough seas and wild weather. Trading carracks were loaded with valuable goods to sell; the *Mary Rose* carried big guns and troops of soldiers.

Great sailing ships like the *Mary Rose* were the most advanced technology of Tudor times. They were constructed by expert craftsmen, using massive timbers, wooden pegs and iron nails. They were enormously expensive to build, and very valuable.

Ferdinand Magellan

Glossary

Amputation Cutting off a diseased limb to save the rest of the body.

Bosun (also spelled Boatswain) Officer in charge of a ship's crew.

Bow Front end of a ship.

Canvas Thick, heavy cloth woven from flax-plant fibres.

Carrack Large sailing ship with a deep hull and three or four masts.

Castle A deck, or small tower of decks, standing on the top deck.

Excavation Uncovering and recording archaeological remains.

Fighting top Platform at the top of a mast, used to shoot down at the enemy and as a 'crow's nest' for a lookout.

Firebombs Jars filled with chemicals that cause fire.

Flagship Ship used by the officer commanding a fleet; it flies his special flag.

Grappling hooks Huge iron hooks, like claws, thrown to catch hold of enemy ships.

Gun barrel Long metal tube; part of a gun.

Gunports Holes cut in a ship's hull through which guns can be fired. Closed with lids when not in use.

Gunpowder Mixture of chemicals that explodes when set on fire.

Heads Toilets on board ship.

Helmsman Sailor who steers a ship.

Hull The body of a ship; the part that sits in the water.

Humours In the past people believed that four liquids flowed round the body – blood, red bile, black bile and phlegm – and that these controlled health and character.

Logline Measured length of rope, used to measure a ship's speed, together with the sandglass.

Glossary continued

Pike Long wooden pole with a small, leaf-shaped iron head.

Pomander Container for sweet-smelling herbs and spices, believed to keep disease away.

Port The left-hand side of a ship (when facing the bow).

Priming powder Fine gunpowder, easy to set alight.

Purser Officer who keeps the ship's money and purchases provisions.

Refitted Rebuilt, improved.

Rigging Ropes supporting a mast or controlling the sails.

Salvage Recovery of an item.

Sandglass Two glass containers joined by a narrow 'neck'. It takes a set time for sand to flow from one to another.

Scuba diving Swimming underwater using Self Contained Underwater Breathing Apparatus.

Sheets Ropes attached to the corners of sails to move them.

Sonar Using sound waves to detect objects underwater; also used for navigation and communication.

Spars Wooden poles from which sails are hung.

Starboard The right-hand side of a ship (when facing the bow).

Tampion Wooden disc placed in the barrel of a gun to hold powder and shot in place so that it can be fired.

Victuallers Traders who supply ships with food.

Watch Four-hour period of duty.

Wristguard Protective bracelet of leather, horn, ivory or stone worn by archers on the lower arm holding the bow to protect the arm from the snap of the string.

Index

For all the stuff you'd rather not know!

You will find loads of free stuff at: youwouldntwantto.be